An Unwavering Horizon

poems by

Gina Williams

Finishing Line Press
Georgetown, Kentucky

An Unwavering Horizon

ACKNOWLEDGMENTS

"Recipe for Man," *Marco Polo*
"Burial at Sea," *Mount Hope*
"Sweet Lorraine," *Foliate Oak*
"Diorama of Ignorance," *Foliate Oak*
"Insanity," *Houston Literary Review*
"The Last Fight He Has Left," *Clementine Poetry Journal*
"The Farthest You Can Go," *Whidbey Life Magazine*/Northwest Institute
   of Literary Arts
"Just for Today," *Snail Mail Review*
"Silver Bells," *StepAway Magazine*
"Flight to Paris," *Red Savina Review*
"With Love from Tehran," *Sukoon*
"Big Pharma, Little Boys," *Carve*
"English Lessons in a Strawberry Field," *Vine Leaves Literary Journal*
"Threads of Understanding," *Whidbey Life Magazine*/Northwest Institute
   of Literary Arts
"The Darkest, Wettest Winter on Record," *Foliate Oak*
"When Enough is Enough," *Fugue*
"A Word for Your Life," *Clementine Poetry Journal*
"Conflagration," *ArLiJo/Gival Press* and *StepAway Magazine*
"Easter Morning," *ArLiJo/Gival Press*
"Recovery," *Synaesthesia Magazine*

Publisher: Leah Maines
Editor: Christen Kincaid
Cover Art: Gina Williams
Author Photo: Gina Williams
Cover Design: Elizabeth Maines McCleavy

Printed in the USA on acid-free paper.
Order online: www.finishinglinepress.com
            also available on amazon.com
         Author inquiries and mail orders:
              Finishing Line Press
               P. O. Box 1626
           Georgetown, Kentucky 40324
                 U. S. A.

Table of Contents

1. Earth / Truth

2. Spirit / Power

3. Air / Love

4. Water / Wisdom

5. Fire / Knowledge

1. Earth / Truth

Burial At Sea

A moody trout is a dead trout,
my grandfather said, his lower lip stuffed
with a wad of wintergreen chew.
Mist flowed across the water as he pulled
the oars gently. I watched every move, took
in every word from my seat atop the
orange boat cushion, feet small
and squirming in the gum boots
chosen from a jumble in Grandpa's shed.

Years later, I recalled those sepia days, all
golden alder leaf spin and reel, fisher philosopher,
cold blue sky, knit cap hug, and hot
sweet thermos tea with a bittersweet backdrop
of Bach's cello suites, so achingly perfect, floating
them along. Thing is, a sullen fish just don't last long,
he'd announce, then spit tar like a perturbed
grasshopper over the bow. Good for us.
Winter seeped in slowly, water beings languishing
in the bracken backwater of lily pads. Too depressed
not to bite, too anemic to fight. Now, I knew,
it wasn't the fish's fault. In faded flannel,
bloated from the bottle, my mother forgot my name.
My father, alone and far away, too slow to run,
lost to a sniper's bullet. Winter does these
things, to fish and men.

A moody trout
is a dead trout is a lost soul is a wandering fool
is a sinking boat. Grandpa taught me to bait the hook,
set the rod, dip the net, break the neck, slit the belly,
peel the guts, turn the boat toward the cove and wait,
wait in the shadows, wait it out.

Recipe for Man

I once created a man out of thin air. I began
with a fistful of light caught as it streamed
 through canvas tent walls
and a lungful of the warm berry smell
of pine needle duff inhaled
on that perfect summer morning.

I was only eight then, but I saved the light
in the penny pocket of my ripped blue jeans,
kept the pine-scented air in the filaments of my hair.

A fire-scorched walking stick carved of maple
became the man's bones.
The sound of an owl hooting
into the black soul of midnight became his voice.
With my mother's spinning wheel, I made tendons and veins,
wove miles and miles of thick, greasy strands
to give his body grace and strength.

The curve of time and a twist of fate
saved in a cigar box beneath a quilt
in the corner of a cedar hope chest
became his heart.
For years and years I collected
bits and scraps of found things,
the poetry of things, like bird's nests and old marbles;
the way aspen leaves flutter, the glint of a salmon
as it rises, a firstborn's hand against her father's cheek,
a letter home, the soft leather of old track shoes,
smell of bread baking, white crust of salt on the collar
of a hickory shirt after a day splitting wood.

These things became the man's strength and spirit.
I waited patiently for a hundred thousand centuries,
anticipating the perfect moment.
Finally, on a brilliant May afternoon,
while hiking in the mountains,

I suddenly saw him there in the rocks.
The idea of him shimmered in the sun,
etched against the basalt.
I positioned my crystal lens just so,
unleashed the light from my pocket
and breathed him alive,
a perfectly imperfect sculpture
of stone and bone and blood
and the poetry of things.
Just as I imagined he would be.

Sweet Lorraine

We never said goodbye.
Now the sink is stacked with dishes,
all clocks in the house set
to a different time. Even the rooster
has stopped crowing.
The baby won't stop crying.

Above the tub, Mom's stockings
hung from the rod, still damp,
as if they'd soaked up all
the grief of the world
and dripped it slowly
down our drain. I tried not to
smell them, but couldn't stop, pushed
one toe to my nose, then ran out.

Now that I'm grown and the folks are gone,
I can only imagine what she was thinking
when they took her away
for treatment behind closed doors
where they shaved her soft
red hair, taped electrodes to her scalp,
tried to zap away demons and despair.

Mom came back one day but it wasn't
really her. How many times was she sent
away before they finally said,
We have no cure for that.

Diorama of Ignorance

How to write about Africa:
he says you start by
washing the elephant.

You never use quote marks.
Each morning a bitter
swallow.

Desire is a yellow leaf, is
a silk-webbed larval case
caught in Chinese breezes,
cornered.

How to write about Mexico:
she says you begin
with chocolate and votives.

Commas should be dashed.
Each day a violent
struggle.

Passion is a pink bloom, is
a cicada raking midnight
trapped by the sea,
lost.

Hope is a crushed seed, is
a golden-feathered songbird
blown off course.

How to write about America:
she says you begin with
toy guns and lost boys.

Sentences must be avoided,
each dream a terrible
curse.

How to write about Russia:
they say you begin
with bullets and grandmothers.

Apostrophes must go,
each generation a lost
cause.

Beyond the County Line

Far afield, wild birds peck with gusto
at the frozen gut pile
left by hunters who scraped the doe clean
at midnight, emptied her glistening remains
along the fence line.

Long winter shadows, ache of brittle branches
uncertain beneath
a cobalt lid of sky.

Crows descend, loud and awkward
from wind-gnarled pines,
bent rays of winter sun
lighting birch scrolls,
their leaf-stripped bones
sturdy in the drifts.

Survival is revealed here,
far beyond the walls we lean on,
outside of fences
and ink-sutured maps defining
yours and mine.

Rising

When the mud room door opens,
I cannot sit still. Could be
planting day, slaughter,
barn cleaning.
I leap up, follow dad's big
rubber boots outside, barefoot.
The soft rattle of seed packets.
In the garden, my feet smile
against warm loam. He
marks rows with sticks,
twine. I squint into the sun,
wrap earth-crumbled worms
around my index finger.

He says, *Let that go and
hold out your hand,*
shakes fat kernels, sweet
'golden jubilee' into my palm.
He spades the holes,
I drop the seeds. Three
kernels each, fill,
tamp with heel.

We sit in chairs now,
his easy, mine desk. The
carefully tilled soil of
my heart is paved
but the mind remembers, and
the memory of that day makes my
soles soften, the petals of my toes
curl with pleasure.
Spring rain is falling, air feels right.

The scent of green.
Somewhere,
near here, perhaps,
small fingers kiss

a fistful of kernels
that will rise into summer
and sweeten the sky
like edible memories.

Insanity

Two madmen are competing for attention
on the evening news. One is adding
Twitter followers at the rate of
2,000 per minute. The other is gunning down
Twitter followers at the rate of
200 per minute. Guess who's winning
The ratings war?

I think of Clarence, the hunched veteran
in room 122, who shipped off to World War I
at age 16 and came back with one
remaining, lucid thought: the sound of
screaming horses is worse than the sound
of any dying man. Blood is thicker
than oil and yet, as it runs from dune to shore,
I can't help but wonder
if it's the sound of camels screaming that
will finally bring us to our knees.

Thoughts While Crossing the Toxic River

Yesterday, a Chinese artist sold
a jar filled with air
from the mountains of France
at an auction for eight hundred dollars.

A cormorant is drying
his wings on an oil-covered
piling above the muddy roil,
beneath an ash grey sky,
instinct his only currency.

Aldo Leopold once said he was glad
to not be young in a future without wilderness.

This bridge is strewn
with the litter of pain.
Blood-stamped gauze, wet
splotches of phlegm, broken glass,
bent needles, one sock stuffed
into a crack.

Toxic currents swirl
toward the sea. A coal train rumbles by.
The cormorant takes off
as I lean dizzily into the railing,
wing-clipped and flightless.

Don't Know it Yet

Gramps is six-and-a-half feet tall and wears
bib overalls everywhere, even on vacation.
His hands are as big as raccoons.
Yesterday, he taught me how to tie my shoes.

I don't know it yet, but Gramps's lungs
are turning to ash beneath the weight of
tobacco smoke, tractor fumes, coal dust.

Don't know it yet, but Gramps is also sick from
grief. Ran over one of his own boys in the drive
long ago. Kids hanging on,
standing on the running boards of the old Chevy,
goofing. One slipped. Gramps turned to alcohol
for pain and television preachers for redemption.
All he got was a mean streak and deeper in the hole.

I'll never see Gramps again,
the next trip an emergency flight east.
He will be dying.
They won't let children in.

If You Wish To Make a Pie from Scratch, You Must First Invent the Universe

Sunday morning, and I'm picking
wild blackberries for a pie
with my son. He's seventeen
now, big hands thick
and rough as paws, yet gentle,
deft around the thorns.

We glean fruit along the path and
because he pours his berries
into mine,
his bucket never fills.

The talk between us is easy,
soft summer air just right,
dark juice staining our fingers.

A lone wasp lingers
on a leaf, and our conversation
turns to the state of things here
on earth.

My son admits—or maybe
reveals/screams/shouts—that he has lost hope
for the world. The planet could do
with about six billion people less
than the seven billion crowding it now—
"At least you had the chance to see it
before it was hopeless," he says, and
my heart shudders.

"Did I?" I ask out loud, guilty.
"Maybe it was hopeless then too,
and I just didn't know it yet."

After supper we'll eat warm pie
on the porch,
watch the horizon glow red,

laugh about nothing,
laugh and laugh.

2. Spirit / Power

The Last Fight He Has Left

I don't mean to listen,
can't help but overhear.
I'm just the help tidying up.
The daughter's strained whispers
are as desperate as wind across the plains.

I hear her pleading with him to repent,
please dad and
it's not too late—hear
her dying father's gruff,
you know I don't believe in that crap
and *leave me be.*
The furnace turns on, drowns out the rest.

When I pass by the sick room
on the way out with my bucket
and rags, he is sleeping.
His daughter has gone.
He looks like a saved man to me,
the way the afternoon light
caresses one bare foot exposed
at the edge of the sheets, the way
the windmill across the dusty yard
spins, turning and turning
in spite of itself,
the leaves on the trees
not moving at all.

The Farthest You Can Go

My son tells me the first thing he wants to do
when he graduates from high school
is get in a car and drive
across the country.

As he tells me this, he just cradles his guitar,
slim fingers picking at the strings,
as if they are questions. *I'd like to check out Maine.*
This sounds somewhat ridiculous. Maine? Why Maine?
An icy wind blows the Chinese chimes on the back porch.
The cat wants in. When I open the back door,
Cold air races across my bare toes
I tuck a piece of tired, loose hair
behind my ear and say,
*I know how good it feels to just get in a car
and go—go on and on. I've done that before.*

But what I want to say is, *Take me.*
Take me with you. I've never been to Maine.
He begins playing this song on the guitar,
and though I know he began leaving me
the moment he left *me*, the very moment
he was born, I still cry for the things I know—
too many things I don't want to be true.

Finally I ask, *Why Maine?*
He doesn't answer, strums a few final chords.
I recognize the song, but can't remember the words.
Later, I will look them up. Later, I will not understand
another part of him.

Because it's the farthest I can go, he finally says.
He puts the guitar in the stand, but my ears still echo the
sounds of him as he runs his hand through his hair and
walks over, gives me a little shove, the way boys do.

Recovery

We're friends now.
Tonight, at a parents' meeting, we stand
together, just like we used to.
Spring sports practice is starting.
Forms need to be signed.

I ask him about his mother—heard she was sick.
Standing this close, the familiar smell of him
reminds me I was young once. My throat tightens.
I begin squeezing odd things in my pockets.

His mother, he says, has the shingles virus, isn't doing
very well. I tell him I'm sorry, that I know how painful
that illness is. He looks at me, quizzically.
Were you with me … when you had it?
Yep, I was… —stop myself
from repeating all things already said
late at night, after the kids have gone to bed.

Heading home alone, rain is pouring,
wipers barely keeping up.
I touch the pockmarks above my
right eye, where the sores left scars,
run my fingertip
along the small indentations on my skin,
over what's left of me.

Ain't The End Times That's Hard

When the tumors at last
bloomed from her breast,
Granny watered the crumbling
red clay dirt with water drawn
from the oaken rain barrel.

There's biscuits to make,
and the men will be home.
How can I tell her
the men were all lost
long ago, gone to war and booze
and blind corners—
leaving, always leaving?

Now fetch me the flour crock,
she says, rinsing her hands
in the cracked porcelain sink,
wiping them on her apron's
prairie meadow. She glances
out toward the empty road,
then sets her jaw, thin lips
an unwavering horizon.

Doing Something

Down along the lava coast, we turn in
at power pole 67, bump along
the rough road marked with white stones.
Little bob-necked birds
peek at us from behind dusty shrubs.
The sea trembles against the horizon.

We descend, and as we step from stone to sand
into the fragrant, gentle peace.
he appears beneath the palms.
He knits in the shade in a frayed beach chair,
long, thin legs crossed primly,
his emaciation etched on a sun-cured
canvas, painted engraving cool sand.
He knits and knits and purls and knits.

Beneath the palms,
pastel yarn winds across
bony thighs, needles crossing, clacking a thin,
easy beat, fibers twisting like nerves.

As we go, I ask.
For the AIDS babies, he explains, softly,
needles never pausing.

Easter Morning

incense rises
from the hands of old men
who insist god is here,
right here in this place
as easter ribbons flutter
from the beams,
light breaking
through stained glass.

i dip my fingertips
in holy water,
toddler balanced on one hip,
lower my head,
mark the sign on my face and his.
he flinches, wipes the drop.

as i pause,
scan the crowded sanctuary
for an empty seat,
he looks toward the altar—
points at the crucified christ
as if seeing it for the first time
and screams, *mommy! look!*
get that man down!

Reincarnation

Came back as a bean, a beet, gleam, a drop of rain.
Slipped and fell,
woke up a rain shadow, a wind, a whistle, a train.

Went off the tracks,
came back as a rail, a rock, a clock, a pill,
a winter chill,
a stalk, a staff, chaff, a sack of grain.

Returned as a boy, a stick, a ball. Oh!
The bouncing, bouncing, bouncing!
That life of bouncing.
Bounced to shreds,
came back as a leaf, a whip, a star, a vein,
a starling, a step backward.

Woke up as a weasel, a whorl, a sinkhole,
a sewer rat, a shrub, a grub, a brush wet with paint.
Felt good, stroking the canvas with my face.

Left as a windmill, came back a stork, a trowel,
a tulip, a mole, a glut, a gut, glutton, a
kitten, a rattle,
a brick, a storm, a wave, a wind, a whirligig,
a crock, crook, a cane.

Died alone, came back as a hive, a horse, a healer,
a mite, wisp, whisper, wink, a wrinkle, a knee, stiff with pain.

Flamed out, came screaming back a beam of light,
a laugh, a cry, a virus, a curse, a pox, a slug, a scar,
a yellow car, a stop light,
and then,
returned as a wish, just one, floating, impossible, un-grantable,
wobbling, spinning, swirling,
orbiting until the end of time
around your brain.

Rave at the End of the Nuclear Summer

A single letter inked on a scrap of newsprint
clings to a dying wish weed. It flutters desperately,
the last font bending against a bitter wind, bombs silent.
Voices silent. Everything silent,
except for wind and wandering heartbeats.
Language languishes here where scorched tongues and
melted skin cannot fathom such delicacies.

Cannot speak of, cannot speak.
Torches blow soot against cave walls. Shivering nomads
mumble empty phrases into starless night.

Navigation impossible

until the rattle of bones and tap of sticks on stone sends shivers;
a reminder, a remembrance.

Knee joints bend. Toes dig into sand. Fingers grip

and then, the vocal cords begin to hum again,
calling out the meanings as if auctioneers, the hard cliff
edge of *el* and *em* and *bee* and *ar* returning.
But first, before speaking, before letters, before cave wall sketches,
they dance, lighting the fat beneath the fuel with their voices spark,
conjuring spirits by leaping into night,
shaking emaciated, greedy limbs to carve it out.
It begins with sound, with a solitary cellular beat, just one.
Thump.

Then three. Rat-a-tat.
And goes on from there, forever, just because.
Claws on coral, gills in gravel. It goes on and on, somehow.
In spite of everything, even you.

3. Air / Love

Just For Today

We head into the mountains
before dawn,
me shotgun.

I'm daddy's 'boy,' just for today,
allowed to use the hatchet
as wood chips fly like bees
off saw teeth.

Alder trees drop echoes
through the forest.

We share donuts
on the tailgate.
I sip from a green
thermos cup.
Real coffee, not cocoa.

Later, at home, we will split and stack
the sweet, damp logs.

I'll show off my new muscles,
take off my blue knit cap,
let my hair fly in the breeze,
hope I'll never be tempted
to settle for anything less
than this.

Spilling the Urn

He didn't mean to.
She wobbled there, on the roof,
trying to hang on,
balanced against
the rack for a good minute.

Until the left front tire hit a rut
and off she flew, into the median,
spilling out of her shiny new
copper urn
in puffs and whiffs,
liver dust, kidney soot, heart smoke,
shattered bones of longing
rising above the freeway.

It's usually the coffee mug or
a sneaker that's left there,
forgotten in a flurry while the
truck is loaded, but this time,
her gritty remains remained.

No choice but to scoop what's left
into a coffee tin with
the old camping shovel
as heads turned, stalled traffic slowed
to a crawl, sun set, and he finally
had her beside him again, the
important parts anyway,
shotgun, for the long,
silent trip home.

Silver Bells

Santa Claus doormen are still out at midnight
When I scoot ass-first off the hotel bed to piss.
From the window, I can see them
doing deep knee bends to keep
warm. Steam rises from underground vents.

Hours before, the pedi-cab driver ate cold falafel
as we lingered over lemongrass martinis
and pad Thai and sipped wine & burned
our conjoined esophagus on kung pao chicken.
A fat baby tossed crackers and cried.

I teeter into the bathroom to
clear my thoughts over the drain
about what I've got. And what I don't.
In the morning, we grope cloud-headed
In sunny fields of thousand thread-count
Egyptian cotton.

We marinate there,
our indulgence smelling of sperm and spilled
wine as the Santa doormen trade red hats
for black ones and go on, opening doors, pushing
buttons, pocketing bills, shuffling bags
wanting, waiting, shivering,
like all of us, until spring.

Blended Family

Daughter pretty
not my daughter my daughter
Sons handsome
not your sons your sons
ours, us—
the whole of them,
bones strung and strumming
voices harmonic rising
humming, silent and singing,
speed of sound a
defining equation
the golden record,
eternal flight.
Parents divided by kids,
not this, the Fibonacci sequence,
essential triangle.
What is the equation
for the speed of silence,
square root of love divided.

If It Wasn't for Me, He'd Still Be Dreaming

When I told my dad I wanted to live forever,
he said, *Just wait 'till you get to be my age.*
Then you'll wish you were dead.

I was eight. He was twenty-eight.
He was always joking, never kidding.

He'd sing, *The worms crawl in, the worms crawl out*
We'd sing, *The worms play pinochle on your snout.*

If it wasn't for me, maybe he'd still be laughing.
He could be a retired Navy captain,
a college professor. If I hadn't
shown up when he was too young to stop me,
maybe he'd still have dreams.

I remember the day he broke. When he
came home that night, there wasn't any
air left. He was a popped balloon. All of
his edges sagged.

When a man can't do it on his own, it
puts notches in his spine, bends him,
twists him up like knotted wood.

He'd sing *Fifteen men on a dead man's chest*
We'd sing *Yo-ho-ho and a bottle of rum.*

Dad cut his leg sawing lumber
for a playhouse when I was five,
before he lost his job,
before he started over digging ditches.
I looked on from the sandbox, sorry for his hurt
as blood bubbled to the surface. I thought
it looked like blackberry jam. And then I thought,
He's real. He's a real man.

Just an Ordinary Tuesday on Earth

I recall a moment around noon,
a heavy man sighing inside the elevator going up.
Why, WHY? he said, into a tiny microphone
held unsteadily near downturned lips.
Because I love you, I said, but not to him, to you.
To him, I said, silently, *I'm sorry.*

And the sun came out today dispelling the gloom,
glinting off gold teeth and silver-tipped canes and spokes,
all kinds of spokes—cartwheeled, bicycle-tired,
wheel chaired & otherwise, shiny and loud
—and the earth tilted and spun and shouted.

A woman on the corner screamed,
Don't you tell me what to do! A man
selling Himalayan dumplings in the square whispered,
Namaste, Namaste. A yellow crane lowered steel beams
into an empty block as sunbeams streamed and slanted
between layers of brick and illuminated
the iridescence of intimate pairings of pigeons dining on crumbs
scattered between park benches.

Now, I curl into a chair on the porch
as the sun begins to set. Children are striking out
at the ball park. I hear them laugh
as their parents cry out, frantic.
Chimes sway and gong above the fray,
repeating the low harmony of what was once
a well-tuned planet, maybe still is for a short while yet,
a song of songs. Birds call out, preparing to roost,
twittering and trilling, and finally a flock of crows crash-lands,
cawing, in a nearby cedar.
After a supper of catfish and fried corn we dance in the kitchen
as the day dims, and finally curl together like pairing snakes,
all skin and heat and tail, intertwined, tethered by tenderness,
windows flung open, the scent of green seeping in,
unbearable and light, lighter than air. Yes, yes, the sun,

that gorgeous, flaring, insanely jealous and flamboyant orb;
that brave and beautiful star,
hovering improbably and perfectly close
and impossibly, exquisitely distant,
came out today.

Flight to Paris

When the oxygen runs out,
Grandma slurps at the thin air
around her. *I'm gettin' woozy*
she gasps.
Then, *I never went to Paris,*
tremoring hands gripping the empty plastic
tube, the lifeless lifeline.
Don't wait to go to Paris, don't
wait for anything.
I'm speeding her home,
the tank having run dry
at a family picnic. In a half
hour or so, she could pass out,
her heart could be strained
and I feel strained too,
somewhere deep inside,
each red light a siren screaming,
It's over
every green light
wailing,
don't wait, don't you dare wait.

When Summer Tastes Like This, I Think of You

The way the sunlight
is angles through the pines,
a sensual tangle
caught up and spinning
in the aspen leaves,
reminds me of that dare,
of us, laughing,
stripping down to nothing,
stashing our clothes in the rocks,
splashing at the river's edge.
Reminds me of kissing huckleberry
juice from the crooked corners
of your mouth, wrapping up
in the salt of your warm, brown skin.
Reminds me how simple we thought
it would be, nothing but pleasure.

The way the clouds
are piled up just now, lingering
above the trees,
bruising the sky with the purple tinge
of a coming storm,
the air hot and thick and sweet,
reminds me that someone loved me,
and I think I loved him too,
before summer ended,
before he went one way, and
I went someplace else.
No reason why,
except that we'd agreed
it was nothing,
just a summer thing,
meaningless. If only I'd known
that summer would never
ever stop tasting like this.

With Love from Tehran, Now Let Me Say: *Goodbye*

I sent Siba a Michael Jackson poster
but she never got it. The censors,
she wrote, probably took it. She would
have loved a stack of American magazines.
She told me not to bother.
They'd take those, too.
The envelope is still so white.

When I close my eyes I can remember
parting it with the letter opener, carefully,
anticipating Siba's neat script in dark ink
on the thin, sky-blue, air-mail paper.
This time, though, the tears came fast.

We'd been pen pals for months,
Siba already in college.
She encouraged me to study hard.

"I love going to school. Of course it is difficult
and you should try hard. Geuthe Institute
where I was studying German is closed
while the war is so hard. Everything in our life
is affected by the war."

400,000 dead, 750,000 wounded.
Babies blown up, blistered by mustard gas.
Neighborhoods evaporated by missiles,
the War of Cities raging on and on.

I climbed the old fir tree in the pasture,
to the highest place I could reach, hidden
in the branches, where I could feel the wind
bending the trunk. I didn't come down until it got dark
and someone yelled for me to come inside.

"You wanted a family picture," she wrote.
"I'll send one as soon as possible."

The British sold Sadaam masks and
suits. Americans sold recipes for chemical weapons,
Russian scuds raining down all night long.
Postmark: Tehran, 1985.
The green-and-purple stamps
depict two bearded, turbaned men. My
name on the front, addressed to our rural route
so far away in Oregon.

"I'm sorry that I have not write so long.
In fact I had a bad time and have now.
We are not in normal situation. I'm talking
about war. Many people has been killed and I
don't know whether I'm alive tonight. But if I'm
alive, I am always here and can receive your letters."

Generations of brothers missing.
25,000 dead in one day.
Desert trenches filled with the stench of hate.
Motherless children left to die in the street.

I never heard from her again, still feel the ache
sometimes, of wondering.
She wrote out her alphabet
and some words in Persian—"love" and "hello"
and "your friend" along with the translation.
In English she continued,
"I hope you always live in peace and health,
your perpetual friend, Siba.
Now let me say: خداحافظی"

Trading Candy for a Prayer

Her habit was so fierce,
she even smoked in the shower,
kept an ashtray on the edge of the counter,
would poke her lips and one dripping arm
out of the curtain to get a drag.
She sent me to the market
a couple times a week with a note
and a wad of cash so I could buy her smokes.

This was okay then, I guess.
I doubt I'm the only kid who ever hoofed it home
with cigs and butter for mom,
but I wanted to toss that pack of sticks
into the creek on the way back.
She woke up coughing every morning,
lungs full of tar. Maybe she thought
nobody noticed those brown-and-blood-spotted tissues
spilling out of the trash.
I didn't understand then why she couldn't just stop,
why she sent me to the store
for something that made her sick.
How could she not know how much I hated
helping her die?

I never ate the penny candy
she let me buy with the change,
threw that into the creek instead,
an offering, perhaps, a crude prayer,
watched it float downstream
until it disappeared.
Then I'd turn toward home,
walking too slowly, imagining the cigarettes
lighting themselves, burning little holes
in the brown paper bag.

Big Pharma, Little Boys

The school calls just before noon.
to inform me
my son is hiding beneath his desk,
insisting that he is not a boy, but a walrus.

When I pick him up, he is crying a little.
His eyes are as sad and heavy
as stones that won't skip.
All but three buttons
are missing from his shirt.
The counselor says
he chewed them off.

On the counter at home,
multiple diagnoses line up
in bottles. How many drugs
can a young brain take?

Is it the yellow pill for sitting still
that put him over the edge?
Or was it the green-and-white-striped anxiety
pill that did that?
Or the blue pill for depression,
the white pill for sleep?
Where's the peace pill,
the *it's going to be okay* pill for me?

I hold him on my lap, rub his back, ask him,
"Are you still a walrus or are you my sweet boy now?"
He only shakes his head no,
twisting his fingers, the down of his hair
smelling of fear and crayons,
sweat and glue. He has drawn squiggle
lines on his hands with an orange marker.

An hour later, something sets him off
and he rages, uncontrollable,

locks himself in the bathroom.
I'm pleading with him to open the door.
He's throwing things, yelling, his small,
angry voice rattling the windows, scraping
more layers from my heart.
I pick at the lock with a pin from my hair,
I'm calling out to him, begging,
"Please, please open the door,
please." I can't get the door to open
and it is suddenly too quiet,
only the sound of my own panicked voice now.
Finally, I break in, find him hanging
in the corner, face purple,
neck tied up in the curtain cord, gagging,
wedged between the window sill and toilet.

I lift him, untangle him as he gasps for air,
his little body light as whispers. I can't
get my legs to move, am shaking as
I hold him there on the bathroom floor, tell him
I'm sorry, so sorry, rock him
in the soft, grey light, promise him
with my lips on his cheeks, my arms
wrapped tightly around him,
that I'll never give up, that someday
I'll know exactly what to do.

Picking Berries

The baby is standing at the edge
of the blackberry patch
in just a diaper and little sneakers,
summer air soft as butter.
You smile watching him,
his chubby hand reaching, fingers fumbling
around the fruit, fat fists grabbing.
You show him how to toss berries into a pail.
They land with a soft thud.
You forget about berries then, get lost
in trying to memorize every detail of him.
You push it all deep
into yourself, like how his hair
is the same color and texture
of a dandelion bloom. The way his cheeks rise
below his wide, blue eyes, how the little rib bones
push outward against his belly with each breath.

You memorize the indent
at the center of his chest
where his sternum catches his heart, admire
the arc of tiny lips, how they appear
etched onto his face. As you focus
on his lashes' blond fringe,
shoulders' curve,
mall bones of his spine,
he suddenly seems utterly perishable,
as if in the heat too long he'd rot.

You close your eyes,
just for a moment, push
the sudden feeling of loss away,
breathe in all the precious details,
inhale them to keep forever, and just then,
the baby screams, his hand
closed around a wasp
stinging his palm, and the poison,

knowing rushes through you:
something will get him,
something will.

Nurse Tree

for C.

Winter gusts punch ancient cedar.
She sways, groans, heartwood cracks.

Wind moans like a wounded creature,
blasts from the north.

Sleet needles her face,
ice frosts tired branches.

Snow quilts a thick blanket
atop her shivering roots.

In the dead of night, a final, brutal shove
sends her crashing

atop the forest floor. A violent tumble—
limbs thrash, earth shudders   silence.

Morning ribbons through misted canopy
like prayers. A varied thrush flutes in the treetops.

Fern spores drift into her pores.
Seeds swell against her knots. Fungi soften her edges.

Infant trees will sink tiny roots
into her nourishing flesh.

Rain pools along her edges.
A rabbit takes shelter beneath her trunk.

She is the sum of what's come before,
a gift to the future.

A giving bridge
across the river of life.

4. Water / Wisdom

Lullaby for Mom

This old woman is wringing her hands.
What time is it, where did my husband go?
I put my hand on her shoulder,
tell her time is in a better place,
though I don't believe it. I tell her
love is right here. This, I know to be true.
She lamented once that she didn't
know me very well.
I replied with one of my only private truths:
It's okay, no one does.

She calms as I settle her down
in her favorite chair,
the one with the stuffing pulled out
so her feet can touch the floor.
Dreams crease her brow
as I stroke her hair, rub her forehead
with the edge of my thumb,
hum a familiar song,
just like she did way back at the beginning
when time was young,
back when she really knew me, once.

What Lurks

Bubbles escape his mouth like flies
as fishermen with tangled lines spit chew,
tell jokes about tits and bulls.
Will I kiss him again?
Wives line the shore, straining to see
around the last bend while
free range cattle shit on the highway.
A bicyclist collides with a minivan
on a blind corner.
The boy in his Dad's Ford crosses
the center line.
One shoe drifts by.
Now the wives are frantic,
knowing what's good can't last,
wondering even while dreaming,
what will erase our sun? What
will trigger our extinction?

Boulders make bets on his skull.
Angry stones bloody his shins
as he tumbles into rapids.
The upturned boat drifts.
Crows laugh from tangled branches,
lungs tighten, skin pricks.
And then I find him laughing,
shoeless, dripping,
limping down the tracks,
paddle in one hand, fedora cocked,
grinning like a cat with too many lives.

We Hadn't Yet Learned How to Kill That Kind of Fish

For long weeks in summer I ran with a pack
of cousins. We'd take Grandpa's dinghy
out into the bay, jeans rolled up,
sunlight splashing on the waves,
the Puget Sound all thick and green
and dangerous.

Most days, we just rowed,
imagining what lurked,
our little boat bobbing in soft swells.
One day without asking
one of the cousins and I grabbed
poles and bait. We thought
we were brave and smart.

We shouted with excitement when the pole
bent hard, reeled up a baby flounder,
its eyes half-metamorphosed across its face,
gills gaping pink and desperate
against the smooth, white belly.

Panic set when we couldn't get the hook out,
when we realized we hadn't yet
learned how to kill a flatfish.
Grandpa taught us what to do with a trout,
how to kill it quick by snapping the neck.
Never let anything suffer, he said.

This flat thing couldn't be gripped.
We put it in a pail, rowed back to shore,
hauled the bucket, pole, fish and all
into our great grandmother's cabin
in search of killing tools.

Bucket water bloomed pink as we
smacked at it with spoons, knives, ladles,
bashed its tiny skull with handles of things.

Grandma came in and screamed at us to stop.
She put her apron to her mouth and began to weep.

The fish flopped half-dead until uncle
stabbed it through the head.
We hadn't thought about the killing part.

Song of the Last Mariner

Last time I saw Carl he had a twelve-pack
of Pabst in front of him,
and a splintered guitar with a missing string.
He took a swig, leaned back,
belted out an impossible line of *Irish Rovers* songs.

He was a seafaring man,
played long ago in a Navy band.
Carl's blind now, feeling his way around
on cords and wires and twine he's strung.
The instrument of life is playing him these days,
as it will us all at the end, as we're led along
following the sounds, turning toward vibrations,
trying to feel our way home from the bar after midnight,
no northern star in sight.

Now he's twisted himself around the invisible hum
of strings and lines, listening to the fervent commands
of radio preachers, waiting
for the good Lord to restore his sight.

A bitter wind's blowing across the desert tonight,
blue half-moon rattling in the willow thicket,
a man out there adrift with nothing to guide
but the howl of minor chords,
Jesus nowhere to be found.

English Lessons in a Strawberry Field

The woman does not speak
until noon. She is small and thin,
her face soft, eyes too creased.
The smell of smashed berries
and earth and sweat rises.
I watch her hands fly.

The lunch horn sounds. The sun is high and hot. I pull a sandwich
and a mason jar of milk from my backpack, push my hat down low.
She sits cross-legged four feet away, slowly
eating rice balls, sipping from a small thermos.

There are other kids my age scattered around, telling stupid
eleven-year-old jokes, throwing bread crusts at each other.
She looks up, points at my jar of milk. "What name?" she asks.
When she smiles, I can see one black tooth.
"This?" She nods. "Milk." She repeats it, "Mirk."
"No, miiilllk." We laugh, and so it begins,
new words and pointing—
sky, grass, cloud, spider, sandwich, apple, rose.
"Me, Rose Vu. From Saigon."

At home, after supper, my dad puts on his old reel
movies taken in Vietnam, his war
flickering in one dimension.
We sit in the dark eating popcorn,
laughing at his silly mustache,
how skinny he was then
in his white sailor's uniform.

But now I think of Rose
as fighter jets take off from the aircraft carrier,
the *Victory at Sea* soundtrack swelling in the background
on our old record player.

I think of how her hands flew, how she never dropped a berry.
I think of new words to show her tomorrow.

On the Wing

'Long as decent weather holds
Bob will unroll his tattered sleeping bag,
bed down beneath the wings
of the biplane
he calls *Stella Blue.*

He's brought her to the local strip,
makes a little cash giving rides—agrees
to take me up so I can see
for myself before writing a piece
for the weekly rag.

Prop spins and the machine roars to life,
floats into the sky
with a sigh and a bounce
as the ground gives way to green and gold canvas.

Ain't getting' rich off it,
Bob says later, a direct quote for the week's news.
Covers the gas, keeps me free.

As I turn my car to go back, I see
flattened areas in the grass
where Bob sleeps
leaving barely a mark upon the earth.

Cracking the Lens

Just before dawn,
flannel-shirted fishermen hustle
on the docks,
filling their tanks with diesel
and coffee.

An arctic loon ripples
the glassy water with a silent dive.
Halyards clang
like Tibetan chimes.

Fog blows in, erasing the horizon,
swallowing the marina whole,
leaving ghosts to wander the pier,
their hollow boots knocking thin rhythms
against ancient planks.

A rough-bearded man
in an orange watch cap
glides by, standing upright,
on a rusted bicycle
with no seat.

"If you take a photo of me, you'll
crack the lens," he shouts in my direction,
then flips a wheelie and disappears
behind the crab shack,
laughter spilling out
onto the deserted street
like spawning gravel.

I linger at the water's edge,
fishing for ruined light,
a stranger to tides
and old ways
as tie ropes are flung
and boats chug

toward deep water,
the hour of the pearl
slipping beneath the waves.

Threads of Understanding

This is what connects—
a fragile red capillary
of understanding
twining as a pea shoot,
moonward,
pulsing against a silver tide,
unspoken cord.

Heron's wings,
silver thimbles,
sealing wax;
The poetry of things,
skipping stones,
salmon bones;
Seed pods and wool scraps,
wooden boats.

These binding things
connect, comfort—
soothing as salted wind on waves,
owl spirits calling,
careful stitches healing
wounded cloth.

5. Fire / Knowledge

Late September

I'm watering green pumpkins and late-ripening corn
in the garden when the butcher arrives
in a dirty white van full of knives, chains,
pulleys, ropes, bone saws—and a rifle.
Buckman Mobile Butcher, From Slaughter to Steak!
is spelled out on the side of his rig
in faded red script. My dad, in overalls
and boots, baseball cap, thin blue flannel shirt,
leads him to the steer relaxing under the walnut tree.

The young steer we named *Spot*
looks at us blankly, blinking flies from his face.
I watch as the rifle is placed directly
onto Spot's skull, watch the butcher pull
the trigger. The gun has a silencer and pops
softly, much too quiet to be deadly.
When the gun goes off, there is a moment
of time sticking, a split millisecond—a tiny
switch-flip between existing
or not. In this moment the animal doesn't fall,
only teeters a little, still upright, and maybe,
I think, maybe there is no bullet.

A half-moo escapes the still-chewing mouth
as the cow's eye nearest me widens, staring into mine,
and I wonder what he thinks of me at that moment,
me just standing there, arms dangling,
watching him die. Then his legs give way
as he collapses onto his side. His tongue slips out.
One eye keeps staring. His tail twitches twice.

I'm called in from the barn for dinner
not too long after slaughter day,
freezers full, the house
smelling of onions and broiled beef,
kitchen steamy from boiling potatoes,
baking bread, frying corn. A prayer of thanks is said.

Then, as knives and forks are raised,
my dad doesn't mean to, isn't trying to
start something, *Oh, look*, he says.
There's a spot on my plate.
The words just fall out.
We all stare at our steaks,
forks suspended.
It suddenly feels like the teetering moment
in the pasture, and my little sister starts wailing

Mom, grim-faced, takes the steaks
with names away, puts them out of sight.
There are barely enough potatoes and corn
to go around now, but even the vegetables
are eaten slowly.

A smear of blood still clings to the edge of my plate.
I hide it under a crust of bread.
The pigs are getting fat.
There are too many rabbits.
By Christmas, there will be newborn lambs.
Soon, the butcher will be back
and I know it's much too late
to ask why.

It just is, that's all.
It just is.

The Darkest, Wettest Winter on Record

This morning the weatherman
said we've had forty-nine days of rain
in the last fifty-seven days.

When the squirrels chased my tires like dogs
back in September, I knew we were in for something.
Winter is like a drinking contest.
Who will be the last man standing?

At times like these the only hope
is to pick fleas and pretend we are Russians,
bundled in piles of fur and drinking vodka by candlelight,
selling secrets to the Nigerians, and
digging holes beneath the snow, just to keep warm.

We'll have beans and caviar again for supper.
We've just enough money left for milk chocolate.
The coffee is getting cold. On the news a stranded calf
is being blown by the force of rotor blades
across the ice to the lakeshore.

We sit on the couch and cry. It's too wet outside and cold,
and we have to keep the squirrels in the house
to keep the fleas off.
I will find them eating the crumbs in my kitchen.
It's cold and damp in the ringlets of my favorite wig.

By midnight, we will have sixty days of rain to mourn
and the vodka will be gone. Where is my fur muff?
Where will we go from here?

Let's plant the beans, fry catfish for dinner,
listen to the branches, tuck in the worm ball of children,
kiss the weather man goodnight,
and sleep it off until a later time,
hope we wake in spring.

Street Smarts

Under the bridge where the homeless camp,
a man in a black knit cap and torn army-green kilt
is demonstrating kung-fu, or perhaps it's karate.

One of his eyes is swollen shut,
black and purple as the storm clouds.
A gusting wind rattles the pane.

Joggers, bent into the weather, trot along
the river path, oblivious. A spotted dog in a little yellow
coat darts unleashed around the man's ankles
as he spars, alone.

I sketch a leafless tree on a notepad
and remember the rent is due. I am out
of bread and eggs, but there is plenty of wine and butter.

The thin glass is streaked with rain and shudders
with leaking cold. Wind whips the branches as the street fighter
surrounded by a motley crowd leaps into the air,
spinning, kicking, jabbing.

I don't know how to fight, wouldn't know how
to kick my way out. The dog smiles as he detects a threat,
nips at the calves of an invisible opponent.
The man runs towards a bridge pillar, kicks,
flings himself into a perfect backward flip,
lands on his feet like a cat.
He curtsies, bows as if on stage,
his friends high-fiving, clapping.

The man bums a smoke and lights up, wipes
sweat from his face, points downriver,
as his small audience shake their heads no.
He shrugs his shoulders, takes a pull from something
inside a paper bag. A rough-looking
bearded man with a basketball tied to his cart,

a filthy green cloth around his head
puts a hand on his shoulder, leans in for a hug.
The men grab on quickly but don't let go,
a long, hard, tender embrace.
Ninja man waves goodbye,
pats the dog on the head,
walks away across the tracks, dragging on a smoke
in spite of the rain.

I watch the man fade into
the storm. I have plenty of wine and butter,
a warm house, soft carpet. But
I don't have any friends like that.

A Word for Your Life

A spotted fawn leaps across
the farm field at dusk.
You kill the engine and in this rare moment of
pause, August moon rising,
the baby stopping to look you in the eye,
you realize a word for your life is
leaping too, rustling the corn.
Squandered.

Where did it go?
Ears bend in waning light,
waiting in vain
for an answer. You even heard this once,
from your grandmother, toward the end.
It goes so fast.

The red and russet tapestry of earth
billows across the plain
like a golden chute,
the toil of harvest
yet undone.

Fawn fades away,
a mother calling—
sun setting
sky on fire,
a lost horizon,
your sinking flame.

Someday, I'll Be Strong Enough to Fight Back

When Mrs. Brown bends over to help the boy
in front of me, I want to poke her huge
butt with a pin and watch her fly around the room.
I'm a bad girl. When Mrs. Brown tells us that leeches
have 32 brains, I have to sit on my hand
to keep it from whipping into the air.
"Well, guess what?" I want to say.
"My daddy has 52 fists.
I counted them all last night."

When I tell everyone in class I won a swimming
contest, Mrs. Brown sends me to the counselor's office.
The counselor has crooked eyes
and his beard looks greasy. His socks don't match.
He takes a puppet out of a closet and tells me to listen
to it and not him. He calls the puppet Jerry.
I know it's a trick. I see Mr. Ford's lips moving.
Then I know he tells lies, too.

"Why did you lie?" he asks, pretending Jerry is talking
and not him. Sunshine is lighting up a Snoopy decal
on the window behind him. I keep looking down at
his socks, one with blue stripes, the other
plain white. I shrug my shoulders but don't speak
as tears brim against my eyelids.

When Mrs. Brown writes on the chalkboard,
her hand slips sometimes.
The other kids cover their ears, but I don't.
I like the sound it makes. Mrs. Brown bends over my desk now,
smelling of baby powder and coffee.
She has hair on her chin. Her lipstick is crooked.
She bends over and looks at my paper.
She tells me I write like a boy.
I twist a braid in my fingers
and tell her, without moving my lips at all,
"Well, guess what? Someday I'll hit like one, too."

The Day I Learned How to Make Myself Invisible

A chair like that still makes me want to vomit.
The notched arms, slightly indented seat, worn,
varnished oak. The sounds of it, the raw scrape
of metal-tipped feet skidding across the
scuffed classroom floor.

> *That's correct, Miss Whatever-Your-Name-Is.*
> *Now get up here and show us*
> *exactly where Mesopotamia is on the map.*

A face like that still makes me want to die.
The word *Mesopotamia* came screaming out,
spittle-streaked rage, as he began foaming at the mouth,
the way he often did, little white flecks collecting
at the edges of thin lips that curled back against pocked,
stained teeth, thick, grease-smeared glasses
slipping on the ridiculously tiny flaring nose.
My lungs compressed, painfully. Light-headed, I walked
slowly to the map of the ancient world,
pulled from the roller hanging at the front of the room.
I turned and pointed high above my head. "There."

> *Touch it.*
> *I can't. Um, can't reach it.*

Chair scraping, me reaching. Don't blush, don't blush.
Straining, tip-toed.

> *I still can't.*
> *Well, you have to. Hop. Jump if you have to*
> *Touch Mesopotamia. Touch it!*

Spittle flew from his mouth as he yelled
Not knowing what else to do,
I began to hop, desperate, lungs completely emptied.
Finally, one last lunging leap and my fingertip smacked
the bottom edge of that horrible word
while the chair wobbled and I jumped to the side
as it crashed to the floor, while the class,
no longer holding back,
let loose into full-blown, hysterical laughter.
When the bell finally sounded, I walked slowly
to the bathroom, locked the door to the outside world,

closed my eyes, and willed myself to disappear.
And when I opened them, adjusted to the light,
looked into the mirror,
no one was there.

Waiting Room

A harp-playing heron snickered
outside the office window
while the money plant trapped
in a glazed jade-green pot begged
for attention on the desk. A sea
turtle blew bubbles on the harmonica,
ignoring chaos and clattering keys
from his vantage point on the
file drawer shelf. The lobsters,
they never stopped strumming.
The hours finally stopped ticking
when the door opened just a crack,
the river met up with her
hair, and the last wave from the
warming, rising sea swept her far,
far away from there.

All the Flags

You look it up
because you have to,
because you don't know, either
what it means—yours, theirs—
what any flag is all about, really.
You look it up
because the way to history
can't just disappear,
all those squares and strips
folded and forgotten,
cut, ripped, pieced
into stripes, moons, bars—
fields of burning, bleeding stars.
So you look it up
and when you do,
truth lunges at you with knives
(and bullets, grenades, bombs, fists)
and your heart comes unstitched.
How we forget and why—
you should look *that* up too,
but you probably won't,
all the flags strung up
and hoisted
by dirty, fraying, halyard nooses,
limp and tattered,
hung against the muted pulp
of grieving sky.

Conflagration

I went to the museum lecture
to learn something new. The photographer
spoke of his travels to Turkey
with stacks of pinhole cameras
to help the children of Syrian refugees
make something beautiful.
You should too, he said.
Those who say can't *mean* won't.
The whole world is on fire.

Around the corner
a man on the sidewalk convulsed in his
sleeping bag. A puckered old woman
in polka dot pants
unlocked her suitcase from the bike rack
in front of the city library. A blond
boy with a begging sign played
his cello so fiercely the strings curled
and snapped in the wind like cables of a collapsing
rope bridge.

The heater was left on
and I sweltered in the night,
tossed in a sticky web of midnight
daydreams, took a pill,
dreamed at last of killer waves and angry relatives.

Now the morning news tells me a bomb went off
at a bus stop someplace in the far east.
Another plane plunged into the sea.
Those children in Syria are dying from the cold
before the bullets can kill them.

The bus was late. I forgot my lunch
on the counter at home. The coffee pot
at the office sparked and smoked.
I cut my finger on the staple remover. My

spine bends a little further to the left each day.
I'm unprepared for fire or weather.
I bought a sandwich,
carried it around, handed it to a man in rags
shivering on the corner,
flames licking at my boots
as I walked away.

When Enough is Enough

The way my dad prepares
these soda crackers,
you'd think he was a priest
making ready the body of Christ,
removing each cracker tenderly
from the wrapper, setting it carefully
on the green chipped plate, spreading
margarine all the way to the edges, exactly
to the edges—no less, no more—
with a kind of tenderness rare in the sort of man
who drives dump trucks and front loaders for a living,
whose fingers seem permanently cracked and raw
from weather and work.

To watch him eat them one after the other,
spots of yellow grease and flecks of crumbs
clinging to his lips, his eyes closed, face smoothed
with simple delight as he pops
each one in whole—

An unopened can of no-name-brand
mushroom soup still sits on the counter.
This plate of crackers is just the starter,
an indulgence before the main course,
and as my bowl is filled,
I believe I might know
now where soul food comes from, why and how,
sense it being born right here, born again,
on the chipped dish, in my father's hands,
in the steaming bowl, here in our dim, greasy kitchen,
in this small, nothing town on a cold February night,
where enough is when the soup is gone
and the dishes are done, when being satisfied
is as simple as that. Soon,
my childhood will be closed up in the cupboard,
sealed up and put away like plates and spoons
and I'll leave here to make my way, set out

in search of my own shadow,
hoping foolishly for something more.

Gina Williams is a journalist, photographer, former firefighter and gardener. She's a Pacific Northwest native and can often be found rambling in the Oregon Outback, volunteering at the community garden, or on assignment in a far-flung location. She lives and creates near Portland, Oregon. Gina is a Pushcart Prize nominee for poetry and founder of Plein Air Poetry Northwest, a nonprofit organization supporting literary arts and environmental activism.

Much of Williams' creative work is influenced by experience and observation. Over the years, she has worked as a firefighter, reporter, housekeeper, caregiver, veterinarian's assistant, tree planter, gardener, community activist, gas station attendant, technical writer, cocktail waitress, and berry picker. Her most curious on-the-job task: feeding pet meal worms for an elderly woman as part of her housekeeping duties. Most exciting: fighting wildfires across the west. Most rewarding: raising her sons.

An Unwavering Horizon is Williams' first published book of poetry.

CPSIA information can be obtained
at www.ICGtesting.com
Printed in the USA
FSHW010712290420
69597FS